Ten Ways to Safeguard Your Self-Worth

Essentials for a Fulfilled Purpose Driven Life

Free it. Access it. Enjoy It.

FreeIt Self-Development Series

By Judy Babu

Book formatting and editing: Dr Jacqueline N Samuels: https://tinyurl.com/AuthorJNSamuels

Cover design and graphics by Serve and Thrive:

https://serve-and-thrive-academy.thinkific.com/

Website: **www.freeit.org.uk**

Author photo by: KB Captured

Published on Amazon © 2023.

Paperback ISBN: **9798860172418**

Content

Dedication

This book is in honour of God, for His calling over my life to serve humanity with the gifts He has graciously entrusted me with.

To my amazing nuclear and extended family and relatives, together with all my spiritual brothers and sisters in the household of faith.

May this book become a go-back-to manual when life throws the unexpected and you can't hold in what's valuable to you.

Join me as we learn the secrets of safeguarding what's precious.

Free it. Access it. Enjoy It.

Free yourself from the negative whispers; know for a fact that nobody can give you your worth.

- Pastor Judy

Acknowledgments

I have immense gratitude for the following key inspirations in my life.

The Holy Spirit without whom this work would still be an idea waiting to be birthed.

I thank God for my husband Tim for believing in me, encouraging, and creating opportunities for me to grow. He has been a great inspiration and a shoulder to fall back to.

To our son and daughter-in-law who always offer affirmations with words every time they send birthday wishes to me.

My counselling supervisor Marilyn Trew, who keeps me on my toes and helps me get out of my comfort zone.

Bishop John B Masinde and Mrs Persiah Masinde for their spiritual mentorship and cover in shaping our destiny for God's assignment in our lives.

Special thanks for their major contribution to Rachel Walton and Jacqui Gitau for investing in me throughout my journey of becoming a community ambassador Coach and trainer.

To Pastor Ruth Mwirigi who pushed me and publicly raised a demand on the long-incubated dream to write a book and connected me with my publisher.

Sincere gratitude to the individuals who willingly shared their lived experiences and transformations through their amazing testimonials to encourage every reader that *it is possible to Free It, Access It and Enjoy It.*

To all my clients and church family, thank you for according to me an opportunity to serve you with the measure of wisdom at my disposal.

Dr Jacqueline Samuels who has greatly helped and supported me with additional contributions, feedback, experience, and insights into this work. She was able to smell the roses and bring them out by watering and nurturing my heart's desire to self-publish this book.

God bless you all as you serve in your spheres of influence.

Pastor Judy Babu

Foreword

Pastor Judy Babu's ***Ten ways to safeguard your self-esteem*** is an embodiment of her life's mission. The author sees souls living out their potential purposefully.

It is an honour to walk closely with Pastor Judy along the faith journey in married life and ministry where I have witnessed her quiet strength and resilience grow and flourish. I am grateful for the skills and gifts which she shares in this first of many uplifting nuggets.

By applying masterful simplicity in her interactive teaching style, Pastor Judy helps the reader reflect and navigate through the intricate issues of the heart. She effortlessly helps the reader to be discerning and guarded for an emotionally healthy life.

Ten Ways to Safeguard Your Self-Worth: Essentials for a Fulfilled Purpose Driven Life is an eye opener to every reader on the power they possess to take charge of their lives.

By Pastor Timothy Babu

Husband and Pastor in Bible Life Fellowship

www.BibleLifeFellowship.org

Every good gift and every perfect gift is from above, and comes down from the Father of lights, with whom there is no variation or shadow of turning. Of His own will He brought us forth by the word of truth, that we might be a kind of firstfruits of His creatures.

(James 1:17-18)

Endorsement

God does not create a nobody or a worthless person. He has a purpose for every person He has created. Moses thought he was worthless because of a perceived deal that the world had dealt him, but God called him to fulfil God's purpose in his generation.

Gideon thought he was worth nothing because of his family background yet the angel of The Lord calls him a mighty man of valour.

Esther did not think much about herself because for over two months the king had shown no interest in her, yet through Mordecai God calls her to step up to her level of favor and authority and she delivered the Jews from the evil schemes of Haman.

David, who went on to become the benchmark of all the kings of Israel, had been given a false label by his father and brothers - 'keeper of few sheep' - yet there was a champion and a king in him. (Psalm 78:10-72).

I like the way God puts it to Jeremiah; *Before you were formed in the womb I knew you, and before you were born I consecrated you; I appointed you a prophet to the nations.* (Jeremiah 1:5).

That is when God put worth in you, not after you were born, not in school, not at university, not after you got a job and not after you got married and got children. But **before you were born**.

In this book Pastor Judy Babu is taking you through a journey of re-discovering your self-worth if by any chance you could have lost it through one or multiple circumstances in your past.

Read on and step up to your God-given purpose in your generation.

Shalom.

Bishop John B Masinde

Bishop of Deliverance Church Umoja, Nairobi Kenya
https://dcumoja.org/

My personal motto is 'FREE IT'.
I believe we all have something we
wish to disconnect from so we can
live.

- Pastor Judy Babu

Introduction

My passion is sitting with people who know there must be more to life than what is presented by life circumstances. My Mum was a victim of circumstances until she became an answered prayer for Jesus according to John 17:24, ***Father, I want those You have given Me to be with Me where I am***. I witnessed Mum's desperation in seeking and craving for love from a man she had trusted for many years. She would call him Daddy because that's how we addressed him when we were growing up.

My Dad was a gentleman and growing up I knew he was the best Dad because I never faulted him for anything. He would bring shopping home every weekend, easing my Mum the burden of having to go to town and shop for foodstuff. He was smart and intelligent, a man the community esteemed and honoured for his charisma. He was an accountant and a great coffee farmer who many tried to emulate because of his excellent work. Mum was a clerk and they both worked for the same organisation which in their time was called a Sacco. Work colleagues became a thing of the past when circumstances changed for Mum. She enjoyed my dad's company while it lasted.

I have memories of Dad taking pride in having the opportunity to be ferried by the company car and Mum would always challenge him to buy his own. It was not until his retirement approached that he saw the need to own his first car, which brought great joy to the family. Dad's sense of worth came from his position at work as well as people's perception of him. Everyone who encountered him talked about how kind and supportive he was. He had become the community chair in most of the meetings and many appreciated his diplomacy and excellence.

It was only when Mum made a drastic and dramatic decision to quit her job that I became curious about the shift. More so because Mum started drinking, something she had never done in all the years we had known her. She had a drinking buddy who happened to be her cousin and because we wanted to justify why Mum was drinking, we started blaming her cousin for bad influence. Little did I know that drinking was not the problem, she just used it to manage the overwhelming stress that had clouded her life.

By God's grace, I began to empathize and supported her in the best way possible although I battled with shame and confusion. I also experienced grief because I began to lose the mother I knew. I saw my own Mum become a victim of circumstances because life threw her a mismatch of what she had known to be her truth.

Beginning to let go of what one has long considered to be true and sure about oneself can be frightening and disorienting, especially if you have no idea where to begin. Breakthrough can come from identifying a person who can offer the right balance of care and safety with sufficient disconfirmation of one's fixed or false sense of self to effect dissonance that can lead to growth and healing.

My Mum's disorientation and fear forced her to start searching for safety and unfortunately, this left her very vulnerable. To achieve a sense of self and begin to thrive again takes patience, sensitivity, and tenacity on the part of the victim, which was a big challenge for Mum.

Dad was kind and willing to pay for counselling so that Mum could get help in managing her drinking, although he kept threatening her that he was going to leave her if she didn't stop drinking. I vividly remember Dad suggesting that we take Mum to a counsellor whose name remains withheld so that she could tell her why she was drinking. The irony of it is that I was invited into the session, something that to this day leaves me wondering which school that counsellor went to because that was a total breach of Mum's confidentiality. I give credit to Mum for refraining from engaging in the session. It was not until I was left alone with her that she confided in me about what was going on. I felt sorry that my innocence was taken advantage of, but I am grateful that it was not a stranger in the room with my Mum.

I always wished I could have a chat with that counsellor for the opportunity to ask one or two questions. It was important for the counsellor to retain the discipline and safety which the training had given her. It is out of this power asymmetry that I encourage my clients to ask questions of counsellors, their training, as well as any information that pertains to the working relationship. I became aware that from this experience derived my yearning to be of service to my clients, family, the church, and my community, hence the passion to write this book.

Mum died before I could share with her my revolutionary insight that *your worth is not given by a person*.

Dad died before I had the opportunity to share with him my new-found insight on the fact that *worth is not determined by what you do or don't do, it's just 'IT'*.

What I did not give my lovely parents, I want to share with you.

Free yourself from the negative whispers; know for a fact that *nobody can give you your worth*.

TODAY

Free yourself from the negative whispers; know for a fact that nobody can give you your worth.

- Pst Judy Babu

Chapter ONE:

Defining Freedom

Do you sometimes feel like life would be better if everyone liked you? Yet the greater expectation you have the more disappointing it gets. And the more disappointing it gets, the more layers of emotions begin to form, almost like getting into a maze waiting to be rescued. And a big scream of 'freedom', seems to be the only thing that would help.

Freedom is one word I have found to be essential in a person's life. The more you learn to access that freedom the more you will thrive in life.

I have realized that it is very easy to confuse **happiness** with **freedom**. *You can be happy but not free*. This is because *happiness* can be sought after, but **freedom is a state of being that emanates from the realization of who you are and what steals it from you**.

Freedom and *responsibility* tend to be inseparable because the latter is activated when self-awareness becomes evident, and you can finally put a finger on the thing that snatches your freedom. This state of *being* needs you to deal with the found thing that steals it and then begin to enjoy it because it's right where you are. Everyone has an 'It' and the earlier we '**Free It**' the closer we get to our freedom. *What's your 'It'*?

When you discover that Freedom had not left you, that it had only been cluttered, you take responsibility and begin decluttering your mind to access it fully and abundantly.

Freedom is essential, no doubt about it!

In your decluttering, remember not to clutter someone else with what you find out but rather to safely place it under your feet and take your control back.

Make up your mind not to put any stumbling block or obstacle in the way of a brother or sister.

As you empty yourself be careful not to allow certain emotions to be projected on those who caused it. Rather, find a way to manage the specific emotion more healthily so that it doesn't affect your relationships. Remember, you are freeing yourself from any block that stands in your way.

Emptying obstacles standing in your way to freedom and release doesn't grant you permission to take away freedom from others. Otherwise, they will no longer have the freedom to relate with you. *You don't take away from others what you have gained as an essential*.

Remember to stand firm and do not let yourselves be burdened again by the yoke of slavery (Galatians 5:1).

Freedom is a state of being that emanates from the realization of who you are and what steals it from you.

- Pastor Judy Babu

Chapter TWO:

Learn to Detect Need, so it Doesn't Devalue Your Worth

- **When your internal frame of reference is faulty you tend not to know who you really are.**

Knowing who you are, has to do with first understanding that your make-up has no fault. Your default is in how much of your truth you know and have internalized because that is what shapes your perception. You create your own reality from your perception. Begin to internalize the truth and remember your truth may not necessarily be another person's truth.

Detecting needs and understanding their impact on your self-worth is an essential aspect of personal growth and emotional well-being. Below are twelve key points to consider in achieving this, but before that, let me reference a story in the Bible that relates to this in Genesis 16.

Historical examples of people who acted from a position of need and the repercussions of their actions

Genesis 16 records the story of Sarah, Abraham's wife, who saw her slave girl Hagar through the lenses of her need for childbearing. In her desperation to have a child, she consented to her husband having a child with her slave girl. After Hagar had conceived, Sarah's perception of her changed because she saw Hagar as a threat. What Sarah perceived as Hagar's arrogance or pride perhaps should have been just the excitement after realizing her potential in being a mother, after having seen herself as just a slave for so long. However, Sarah's excuse did not warrant her to ill-treat Hagar because in her position she should have dealt with Hagar's attitude in a better way.

Was there anyone in Sarah's circle of influence who might have counselled her to prepare her heart of any possible consequences from her planned action? How many of us fall into similar situations?

Let us examine Sarah's position. God had promised Abraham that he would become the father of many nations. Yet Abraham and Sarah had no offspring to their name. They were wealthy, with no heir in sight, which in their context may have looked like the missing link to feeling worthy or significant. Therefore, Hagar bearing a child who might have been the heir to their kingdom would have triggered animosity and great discomfort.

The irony of this story is that Hagar's internal frame of reference led her to become a victim of abuse at the hands of the people who should have discerned her potential. They should have mentored her into becoming a full-fledged homemaker. It was not until she encountered One who sees us all differently, over and above how everyone sees us, that Hagar was vindicated. He saw her vulnerability, selflessness and sense of worthlessness and came to her rescue.

Reflection:

Sarah's 'helpful' action left her feeling that she was no longer in control of her household and offspring's destiny, which is a need of wanting to feel significant.

Do you think Sarah might have regretted opening Hagar's door to motherhood?

Both Hagar and Sarah were in the drama triangle where both found themselves playing the role of victim. Sarah expected Abraham to rescue her, and Hagar was ready to die in the wilderness. For Sarah, Abraham was not going to get into the drama and so he shifted the responsibility back to her by reminding her that Hagar was in her hands, and she could do whatever she deemed right to do.

Such is life for us too. We are not exempt from such dramas. In our search for significance, we are sometimes quick to blame people for things that have failed, and we end up becoming victims of our circumstances. Until we come to terms with ourselves and realize the power at our disposal to change our circumstances we can easily drown in our sorrow. Although Sarah's decision would not be recommended, she stepped out from a victim position to take responsibility over an issue she had initiated.

Do you think at certain times we need people like Abraham who will push us to take responsibility and exercise the power within?

Hagar was rescued by God Himself. She gave the name *The One who sees me* to the LORD who spoke to her: *You are the God who sees me*, for she said, *I have now seen the One who sees me* (Genesis 16:13).

Read the full account of Hagar and Ishmael in Genesis 16:1-16.

> *Now Sarai, Abram's wife, had borne him no children. And she had an Egyptian maidservant whose name was Hagar. So Sarai said to Abram, "See now, the Lord has restrained me from bearing children. Please, go into my maid; perhaps I shall obtain children by her." And Abram heeded the voice of Sarai. Then Sarai, Abram's wife, took Hagar her maid, the Egyptian, and gave her to her husband Abram to*

be his wife, after Abram had dwelt ten years in the land of Canaan. So he went into Hagar, and she conceived. And when she saw that she had conceived, her mistress became despised in her eyes. Then Sarai said to Abram, "My wrong be upon you! I gave my maid into your embrace; and when she saw that she had conceived, I became despised in her eyes. The Lord judge between you and me." So Abram said to Sarai, "Indeed your maid is in your hand; do to her as you please." And when Sarai dealt harshly with her, she fled from her presence. Now the Angel of the Lord found her by a spring of water in the wilderness, by the spring on the way to Shur. And He said, "Hagar, Sarai's maid, where have you come from, and where are you going?" She said, "I am fleeing from the presence of my mistress Sarai." The Angel of the Lord said to her, "Return to your mistress, and submit yourself under her hand." Then the Angel of the Lord said to her, "I will multiply your descendants exceedingly, so that they shall not be counted for multitude." And the Angel of the Lord said to her: "Behold, you are with child, and you shall bear a son. You shall call his name Ishmael because the Lord has heard your affliction. He shall be a wild man; his hand shall be against every man, and every man's hand against him. And he shall dwell in the presence of all his brethren." Then she called the name of the Lord who spoke to her, You-Are-the-God-Who-Sees; for she said,

*"Have I also here seen Him who sees me?"
Therefore the well was called Beer Lahai Roi;
observe, it is between Kadesh and Bered. So
Hagar bore Abram a son; and Abram named his
son, whom Hagar bore, Ishmael. Abram was
eighty-six years old when Hagar bore Ishmael to
Abram.* (Emphasis mine)

Time to Reflect:

Sarah's 'helpful' action left her feeling that she was no longer in control of her household and offspring's destiny, which is a need of wanting to feel significant.

In what way do you think Hagar might have regretted opening the door to motherhood for Sarah?

Name 3 lessons you have learned from Sarah and Hagar's story and their significance in your own life or the life of someone close to you.

What advice would you give someone going through a situation where they perceive themselves as the victim? How would you help them reframe to shift into solution mode?

BC's testimony

At our first meeting, I wasn't sure how the outcome was going to be. I had never had a 1:1 meeting to talk to someone about a problem, especially someone I didn't know well. It was only when I started sharing my story that I started reflecting on how much I had allowed FEAR to control me. I also became aware of how people's opinions had affected me for a whole year.

My sessions with Pastor Judy helped me gain a lot of confidence. I had believed the lies that I was ugly to the point where mirrors became my worst enemies. I could not look at myself in the mirror. The thought of seeing the beautiful woman I see now was foreign.

My biggest breakthrough was confidence, I was able to break away from fear which helped me conquer obstacles that came my way. Today I am sharing my testimony which is helping and encouraging many other women who have struggled with low self-esteem. My story has become my sermon. Glory to Jesus and Pastor Judy for listening to my problems, praying with me, and helping me acknowledge that nothing was impossible to achieve.

My healing and total restoration were confirmed again two years ago when I met a neighbour who happened to be one of those who troubled and triggered fear in me. This encounter happened when I was serving in my role as a surgical nurse. Rather than reawakening memories of the past, I was able to introduce myself and it was a surprise for him to remember who I was. I didn't have to dig the buried wells of pain because I had recovered. I served him effectively with all integrity, encouraging the others to give him the best care. It felt like in God's calendar the time to prepare a table in the presence of my enemy had surfaced and I thank God that my caregiving preceded anything else.

I am forever grateful to Pastor Judy for spending time to encourage me in my lowest moments. I was able to overcome fear and the feeling of rejection. I have become and an encourager and many are eating from the fruit of my recovery.

BC

Wrong perception will not serve you in ways that allow you to be your best self. It will limit you from achieving your desired goals.

- Pastor Judy Babu

Chapter THREE:

How to Rescue Yourself from Becoming a Victim

#1. Become aware.

Developing self-awareness and understanding your emotions and thought patterns is a gift to your very being. Pay attention to moments when you feel undervalued or inadequate and try to identify the underlying needs that may not be met.

#2. Single out your core values.

Be acquainted with your core values and principles. When you know and are convinced about what matters to you, it becomes easier to recognize situations or relationships that may compromise your self-worth.

Know your truth.

Truth emanates from your belief in what seems to be the reality in your world. Your reality may contradict what everyone believes, remember speaking your truth is the most powerful tool that you have, therefore cling to it, fight for it and manifest it. Truth defines you.

Step out of the drama triangle.

You have power within you that can get you out of self-persecution. Be kind to yourself and learn to take responsibility than depend on external rescue which is not guaranteed.

Become self-aware, always yourself what lead to you being where you are and what resources are available to get you out. Everyone needs some skill sets to get out of the drama of playing victim, persecutor, and rescuer.

Mastering ten core values in safeguarding your self-worth

Everyone is distinct and what one considers as "success" can differ based on individual goals and aspirations. However, below are some pointers that can help boost the different aspects of life:

Resolution: Life has a way of throwing all sorts of things, and unless we are firm and steady in pursuing the desired, challenges, setbacks, and obstacles can easily abort what is meant to bring success to you.

Rectitude: Good morals and a personal ethical framework to safeguard your trust from people can earn credibility, and a positive reputation, which are essential for long-term victories.

Plasticity: Learning from your own mistakes accords you lived experience that can be your lessons in building your future better rather than counting the losses.

Passion: Identifying what keeps you afloat and excited about what you do can fuel motivation and drive, making it easier to remain on the path to your destination.

Regulation: What you consistently do becomes your discipline in managing time and effort, which in turn regulates you when distractions come your way. Find a, routine, and purpose to stick to it.

Creativity: The willingness to expand the horizons of your creativity pushes you to new ideas and opportunities for expansion and growth.

Ongoing pursuit: When you are learning you stop advancing and focus on yesterday's glories. A thirst for more knowledge attracts more insight and education, hence gifting yourself with self-development.

Flexibility: In a world that is ever changing, openness and adaptability to new circumstances is the only tool for positive change. Therefore, embrace change and embrace the newness of what comes from it.

Synergy: A standalone adventure can limit you but when you draw on positive and strong relationships, you can achieve a combined effect that will bear greater fruits or outcome that can impact more.

Thankfulness: Developing a win, win, attitude can propel you to do more. Good is measured by what is deemed measurable and realistic. Every little effort that moves you from where you were previously to a step forward is counted as progress. Be intentional about counting each step up your ladder.

Remember that the definition of success is subjective, and these values can be applied differently depending on the goals and aspirations of everyone. It's important to align your values with your personal vision of success to lead a fulfilling and purposeful life.

- ***Self-perception limits your true worth and ability.***

You are as limited as the knowledge you retain. The more Truth you know and the more you allow it to define you, the less damage is caused on your perception. Remember, **perception** can be changed depending on the source of your knowledge. Establish the right source of your true worth. One question you must always ask if you want to change your perception is, '*Who has written the manuscript for my life and how can I build on it?*

What is TRUTH for you? Psalm 139:14 says You are fearfully and wonderfully made. Isaiah 62:3 states you are a crown of glory and a royal diadem in the hand of God.

Additionally, in Judges 6:15 Gideon says this in response to how God saw him; *Pardon me, my lord," Gideon replied, "but how can I save Israel? My clan is the weakest in Manasseh, and I am the least in my family.*

Wrong perception will not serve you in ways that allow you to be your best self and it will limit you from achieving your desired goals. Most of the time we allow the inner critical voice to take preeminence in driving the course of our life. How you relate to yourself matters more than how others relate with you. People serve you based on what you give or allow as part of you.

Time to Reflect:

1. What perception do you have about yourself?

2. Is everything in your life working out as you expected? Yes / No

If *No*, can you recall what triggers might have created the disconnect?

Note: If there is a feeling of lack, it can often derail our vision and keep us from attaining our Divine purpose.

3. Has what happened to Sarah and Hagar happened to someone you know? How did the person deal with the unexpected dilemma?

4. What are some areas you can help the person work on to release the emotional trauma and feeling of blame that manifested because of the previously mentioned actions?

TODAY

What you consistently do becomes
your discipline in managing time and
effort, which in turn regulates you
when distractions come your way.
Find a routine, and purpose to stick
to it.

- Pst Judy Babu

Chapter Four:

How to Change Your Self-perception

To change your self-perception without blowing your own balloon out of proportion,

Follow these tips…

#3. Know your limits: Your ability to set healthy boundaries in your relationships can help manage yourself. Exercising assertiveness and allowing others to have an opinion does no harm to anyone. Your truth becomes the parameter that keeps you on track.

Identify the right voices: People who value and embrace you for who you are should take the first place in your domain. They are the ones who see the good in you that you cannot see sometimes. They never rest until they hear you acknowledge what they can see as potential. Set the energy you need to surround you because your truth needs to thrive in it.

External affirmation is not always a guarantee:

Depending on external validation or affirmation is setting yourself to fail because people don't necessarily see what you see in yourself. Your inner eyes should be the guiding aid to your inner frame of reference which ferns the belief that you are good enough.

Show compassion: To exercise friendship with yourself, be kind and gentle to your very being. Imagine if one part of your body had a voice to speak, what kind of a friend would it say you are? Embrace imperfections and mistakes as opportunities for growth, rather than as indicators of worth.

Learn to use the two letters: Your inner critic has so much power and the more you exercise to say 'no' especially to your inner critical self, the more confident you become in saying no to others. Focus on giving yourself the first place and remember it is not selfishness. Saying no to things that don't align with your values or needs is an act of self-respect.

Use the award system: Everyone is good in something plus you. Learn to share your victories because those are your testimonies that remind people that you are also human who is in motion and not static. Everyone has something to show off about because we are all a makeup of strengths and weakness.

Lived experience is your tool: You have lived and experienced life therefore you are book that others can learn from. Purpose to open it so many can hear what you have to offer. Your space cannot be another person's space. You occupy because there something about that the universe treasures. Shine your light and don't cover it because it is part of what lights the world.

Give yourself first place sometimes: When you celebrate yourself you teach others to do the same. You are the pace setter in celebrating the glow within you because you are made in the image and likeness of God.

Tell people what they don't know: There are things that people don't know and will never know about you until you tell them. Acknowledge your achievements and successes, no matter how small they may seem. Celebrating milestones can reinforce a positive self-image.

Be your best friend: When things are tough, and you cannot withstand, be the friend that shouts out for help. Sometimes your self-worth is consistently impacted by external factors or past traumas, consider seeking support from a therapist or counsellor can help keep you afloat and regulated.

Remember, recognizing and meeting your needs is not selfish; it is essential for your overall happiness and well-being. By valuing yourself, you can cultivate healthier relationships, make better decisions, and lead a more fulfilling life.

- ***People's labels can easily devalue your true worth.***

People have a way of using their personal needs as bait to manipulate others. Some of them do it unknowingly while others are driven by self-centeredness. Failure to meet their need earns you a man-made label to discolour you, which makes them feel good when they realize you don't feel good about yourself.

You must always remember you are not responsible for people's feelings because nobody makes you feel. Likewise, other people also can never make us feel our feelings because our feelings are ours and they show up within us. We each have our own feelings. So, if someone feels you are not good because you did not fulfil what they wanted you to do, refuse to take on any label because you are not responsible for how they feel.

Saul's self-centeredness in retaining fame and significance made him feel jealous and angry with David. However, David was not responsible for Saul's feelings because his feelings came because of his own needs. Saul refused to acknowledge David as a King because he only knew himself as the King and he wanted everyone to see David as he saw him, just an ordinary person.

1 Samuel 18:8-9 Saul was very angry; this refrain displeased him greatly. *They have credited David with tens of thousands,* he thought, *but me with only thousands. What more can he have but the kingdom?* And from that time on Saul kept a close eye on David.

As you ponder the above scenario, take a moment to reflect on your own life and how your decisions may have been triggered by the actions or attitudes of others.

Time to Reflect:

Who has mistreated you because of your success?

Have you been honoured with preferential treatment or liked more than your mentor?

How has that impacted your relationship with those who were positioned to mentor or uplift you?

Society's limited and incorrect labels

Sometimes labels serve our inherent need for attention and recognition; that is why we fall prey to society's expectations in trying to gain importance. Remember people's label of your worth is based on their understanding of their own level of worth. Therefore, you can never be guaranteed that the standard they set is based on what is true. Could it be just a figment of their imagination of what worth should look like? As you are not a mind reader, you cannot subject yourself to meeting society's needs otherwise you become a puppet for them.

Free yourself and know for certain that you cannot meet everyone's needs.

- ***People place a demand on you based on their own needs.***

If people will only value you because of what you can do for them, it means that your worth has a condition. If you allow conditions set by people to measure your worth, you then become their subject because you must maintain that condition endlessly. Instead, **serve yourself by affirming your own worth unconditionally and quit being the second person to place a condition on your worth**.

In the book of Esther, Queen Vashti faces a conditional offer in maintaining her position as a queen. Her husband expects her to come before a multitude so he can show off her beauty. But knowing that the husband is acting that way because he is under the influence of a drink, she declines and is ready to lose the position rather than become an object of show. Although the leaders think that she might influence the other women in disobeying their husbands on the one hand, her courageous action will help others not become victims of display.

King Xerxes' need to receive accolades from his subjects was fuelled by intoxicating drink. That is why it is important to know who you are and refuse to allow conditions to make you earn what is rightly yours.

This will eventually help you to help others do the same for themselves and get delivered from depending on others in their self-serving needs. Purpose to turn to God who is the Source of everything we need.

Equality is not about meeting a need; equality should be seen in acknowledgment of who a person is. The kingdom of God within us shows equality because of the space we occupy on earth, not just the needs we meet. King Xerxes saw Vashti as unworthy of her position for failing to meet his needs.

Do you sometimes feel you have to keep pleasing people all your life?

David learns this secret and refuses to become a victim of circumstances. He encourages himself in the Lord and commits to make God his dwelling place and the definer of everything he does.

Psalm 27:3-5 encourages us:

> *Though an army may encamp against me, my heart shall not fear; though war may rise against me, in this I will be confident. One thing I have desired of the Lord, that will I seek: that I may dwell in the house of the Lord all the days of my life, to behold the beauty of the Lord, and to inquire in His temple. For in the time of trouble He shall hide me in His pavilion; in the secret place of His tabernacle He shall hide me; He shall set me high upon a rock.*

God has your blueprint. Whatever He says He establishes even when we sometimes find it hard to believe.

Jeremiah 29:11-14a reminds us,

> *For I know the thoughts that I think toward you, says the Lord, thoughts of peace and not of evil, to give you a future and a hope. Then you will call upon Me and go and pray to Me, and I will listen to you. And you will seek Me and find Me, when you search for Me with all your heart. I will be found by you, says the Lord.*

TODAY

Serve yourself by affirming your own worth unconditionally and quit being the second person to place a condition on your worth.

- Pastor Judy Babu

Chapter FIVE:

Raise Your Spiritual Love Detectors to Secure Your Worth

- **_Speak positive words._**

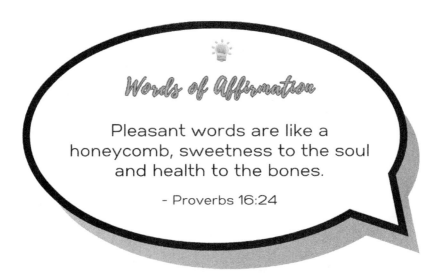

You have exceptional power in your words that can help create your own reality. What you hear yourself saying about you, has more impact than what you hear others saying about you.

You are a cocreator and you can easily shape an image in your mind with words. Words carry with them instructions to shape and define destinies. If you do it to others why not become your own prophetic voice when all the other voices have a negative vibe

Numbers 13:30 declares, *Then Caleb silenced the people before Moses and said, "We should go up and take possession of the land, for we can certainly do it."* (NIV)

In Ezekiel, the prophet Ezekiel was taken by God to the valley of dry bones. There, God caused Israel's dead to rise again, but He did it through Ezekiel's mouth. How?

In Ezekiel 37:7, 10 he says *So, I spoke this message, just as* (God) *told me. So, I spoke the message as* (God) *commanded me, and breath came into their bodies. They all came to life and stood up on their feet as a great army.*

Ezekiel obeyed God's command to speak His Word to the dry bones, and they went back to life. Ezekiel didn't merely speak positive words from his store of encouragement. Rather, he spoke what God told him to speak, and consequently saw what only God can bring back dry bones to life, complete with flesh, blood, and breath.

In the same way, friends, we must let God's Word fill our mouths with what we declare over ourselves. We can't expect God to do to us that which He didn't say. Let His Word be our declaration – and source of expectation. You should always be the loudest voice to your inner hearing.

- ***Speak the Word of God and it will help you recognize if people see you as a treasure or a trash.***

Your spiritual mirror is the Word of God; what it says you are you can become. If you can keep the right mirror in front of you all the time, you can be able to discern the box each person places you in – the treasure or the trash box, and you can choose which box you want to remain in.

The power of choice is in your own perception, and the perception you hold about yourself is in the lenses you see through. Remember the Word of God is your absolute 'Secret Detector' that can help you be assertive and say *no* to what defines you incorrectly.

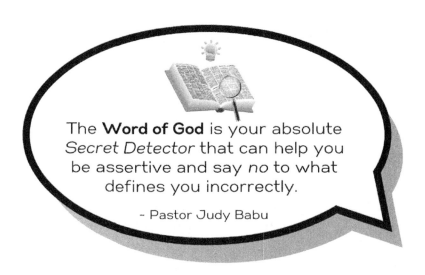

The **Word of God** is your absolute *Secret Detector* that can help you be assertive and say *no* to what defines you incorrectly.

- Pastor Judy Babu

Although Joseph 'the dreamer' was seen as *trash* by his family, he refused to remain in the trash box and chose to see himself through the lenses of God. When he made himself known to his family after they had sold him as a slave, he had this to say (Genesis 45:1-7):

Then Joseph could no longer control himself before all his attendants, and he cried out, "Have everyone leave my presence!" So, there was no one with Joseph when he made himself known to his brothers. And he wept so loudly that the Egyptians heard him, and Pharaoh's household heard about it. Joseph said to his brothers, "I am Joseph! Is my father still living?" But his brothers were not able to answer him, because they were terrified at his presence. Then Joseph said to his brothers, "Come close to me." When they had done so, he said, "I am your brother Joseph, the one you sold into Egypt! And now, do not be distressed and do not be angry with yourselves for selling me here, because it was to save lives that God sent me ahead of you. For two years now there has been famine in the land, and for the next five years there will be no ploughing and reaping. But God sent me ahead of you to preserve for you a remnant on earth and to save your lives by a great deliverance.

Through his journey to self-discovery, Joseph was able to rise above adversity and embrace his true worth. His new mindset and positioning allowed him to deliver his brothers from shame and famine and to restore them in love. God used the episode to reconnect Joseph with his father and restore Joseph's respect in his brothers' eyes. He also met his youngest brother Benjamin who he did not know existed. Reframing and embracing God's nature brings healing and deliverance on many levels.

- ***Encounter and embrace God's Love and save yourself from becoming a victim of the trash box.***

A genuine father has no greater love than to sacrifice His own life for the sake of reaching out to you.

When you learn to receive love from God, you can be able to detect conditional love. Cultivate a relationship with God and soak yourself with unconditional love so that when conditional love presents itself you can choose to ignore it or else share your unconditional love in response. If you cannot get what you need, learn to give it.

Joseph did not get the love he needed from the brothers and so he chose to show it himself; that's what unconditional love looks like. *For God so loved the world* that hated Him by giving His only begotten Son (John 3:16).

- ***Learn to treat yourself better than others do.***

You cannot depend on others to give you what you can freely gift yourself with. If you cannot love yourself then there is no point expecting others to love you. People detect how much you value yourself by what you put a stop to. Teach people how to treat you by the way you treat yourself. No one should know you better than you know yourself.

Paul is very confident about the kind of a person he became that he tells the church in Philippi to imitate him by doing the things he did, exercise what they learnt, received, and heard from him (see Philippians 4:8-9).

He taught them to only focus on things that were true – *Amid many doubts about you, what is one true thing you know about yourself?*

Again, he said, learn to focus on things that are noble – *What are your personal morals that make you who you are?*

Think of things that are just – *How often do you judge yourself instead of being fair and showing compassion?*

Paul would have judged himself harshly because of his past but he learnt to forgive himself and exercise fairness on himself hence he was able to thrive in his calling. Paul encourages us to focus on things that are pure - it is in Christ's righteousness that we are now made right and holy, not of ourselves that we may boast but by His grace. You are not perfect but in Christ you are being made perfect.

Whatever things are of good report – *learn to be grateful each day and focus on what is better and working rather than on what is negative and not working.* Remember that you can only do so much. Learning to meditate on things that are praiseworthy and pleasing in your eyes will boost your esteem and connect you to the other parts of your life. This helps to change our mindset and gives you a shift in perception. It is easier and safer for your mental health than doing the opposite.

If you can learn to exercise the above on yourself, you can also do it for others. Serving people helps you know the different parts of your life.

Self-reflection activity:

In the lens slots below, write down the keywords that resonate from the above discussion.

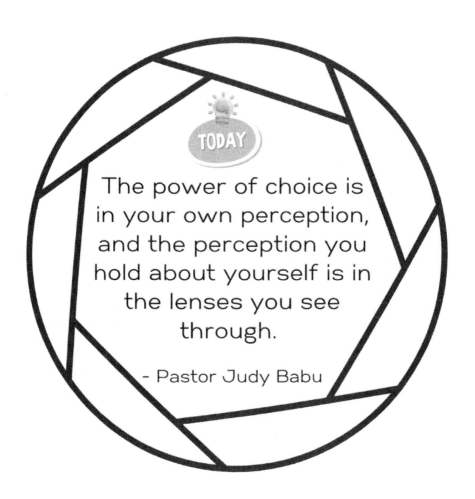

The power of choice is in your own perception, and the perception you hold about yourself is in the lenses you see through.

- Pastor Judy Babu

- *Self-love to empower and resource our own cups so we can serve out to others.*

You can only give what you have not what you depend on. Go back to a stream that never runs dry because that's the only way to keep serving yourself with enough each day. Loving self means connecting with the lifeline of your love resource that is everlasting. John 4:14 states, *whoever drinks of the water I give will never be thirsty again, the water I give will become in him a spring of water welling up.*

The woman at the well depended on the resources that men gave but that never quenched her thirst because she kept looking again and again. She could not give anything because she had nothing to give and so she became a taker to the point of taking what belonged to others. But when she met Jesus the Source of living waters – she had so much love to share with others, even those that conditionally supplied the love she craved for (John 4:15, 28).

Connect with the love of the Father and become a stream that wells out freshness of love that quenches unhealthy cravings that keep people in bondage and needy.

- *Raise spiritual love detectors by loving yourself using God's love which enables you to love others. That creates a ripple effect on you. What you pour out in love reciprocates back to you.*

A disconnection from the source will lead you out to external streams which Is this case will be people. Unfortunately, people can easily switch off the supply depending on how much they want to give. Become a spiritual stream where others can draw from and keep them away from queuing for love – in the wrong streams.

Blessed is a man who delights in the law of the Lord, that person is like a tree planted by streams of water, which yields its fruit in season and whose leaf does not wither— whatever they do prospers (Psalms 1:3).

In the olden days village streams were limited and sometimes only one supply was available for the whole street. Many would find themselves fighting for one stream.

Don't allow desperation to cloud your life. Become God's supplier of unconditional love and let that love come back to you in return.

Raising your spiritual love detectors and securing your worth can be a profound and transformative journey. Here are ten ways to help you on this path:

Soul searching: Reflect on what your beliefs are because your reality is shaped from that. Your reality comes alive in your interactions with others. If you believe God loves you, that virtue will be manifested when you encounter people who may not necessarily love you. Offense may be far from you if you hold onto what is in your love tank.

Cultivate alertness: Always bring yourself to the here and now because the present moment has potential to help you get grounded as well as help you take charge of your judgments and thoughts that can easily sabotage you. Remember because you are precious and honoured in God's sight, He will give everything for you (Isaiah 43:4).

Keep a record: Learn to count your blessings and achievements as a reminder of God's faithfulness. Your test should always translate into a testimony because you are not where you were yesterday because each day is new.

Refill your tank: As you practice showing love and compassion to others, you must put yourself in the circle of recipients because you need to give it to yourself too. Practice acts of kindness, empathy, and forgiveness, both towards others and yourself.

Notice who is in your space: Growth is essential and therefore you must engage in a supportive and uplifting community of friends and family who help you thrive as you help them too.

Treasure spirituality: The physical is good but spiritual practices that resonate with you such as prayer, meditation or spending time in nature will deepen your connection to your spiritual self and the world around you.

Master the critical voice: Develop a positive mindset and practice reframing self-critical thoughts with affirmations of self-worth.

Know your parameters: Learn to define relationships because they are crucial and important. Set healthy boundaries in your relationships because not everyone will understand you. Learning to be assertive and speak out so you may be understood.

Accept your weaknesses: Nobody can do everything. Embrace your imperfections and see them as part of your unique and beautiful journey. Your weakness is what creates room for people who complement you. We need each other in this journey of life.

Love beyond measure: Lift the condition that wants you to pay for love without expectations or conditions. Embrace the concept of unconditional love for yourself and others, acknowledging that we all have strengths and weaknesses.

Remember that raising your spiritual love detectors and securing your worth is an ongoing process. Be patient with yourself and allow space for growth and transformation. Seek support from mentors, spiritual guides, or therapists if needed, and be open to learning and evolving along the way.

Pretty's testimony

For the longest time, I believed the horrible lies people said about me, and my thoughts would work overtime thinking *"People don't like me, I am judged, I am not saved enough, I am not accepted."*

Attending sessions with Pastor Judy has been a game-changer for me. I now know that my worth is not determined by society, but is found in God alone. I have learned that the mistakes I have made in life do not change my worth, because my worth is intact.

My greatest breakthrough was discovering how to dispel negative thoughts, replacing them with the Word of God. Now I can stand before people without feeling inadequate or judged. I can walk with my head high because I know I am a child of God and a confident woman.

My encouragement to someone who is feeling worthless is not to sit there and die, or fall into a pit of depression. You can get your breakthrough by speaking to someone you trust, someone who will lead you to the Truth found in the Word of God. This is the best thing I did.

Pretty

Chapter SIX:

Worth is Not Dependent on Anything Outside of Itself

Do you know your worth?

We often define our worth using someone else's yardstick and understanding.

- *Being liked by others only acknowledges love.*

The fact that someone loves me doesn't mean it's adding anything to my worth. My worth is not dependent on someone saying, "I love you." Therefore, people loving or limiting our love does not diminish our worth in any way. You are the total of your worth and this should be a script inscribed in your heart. Learn not to doubt yourself during condemnation and free yourself from the cycle of second-guessing to try and justify if you are okay or not.

- *5 languages of love. We all resonate with different languages of love from various relationship groups* (spouse, children, family, friends, colleagues, and others).

The concept of the "5 languages of love" is derived from the book *The 5 Love Languages* by Dr Gary Chapman. In his book, Dr Chapman suggests that there are five primary ways people express and interpret love. These love languages are:

1. **Words of Affirmation**: This love language involves expressing love through verbal and written affirmations, compliments, and words of encouragement. People with this love language feel most loved when they hear kind and appreciative words.

2. **Acts of Service**: This love language centres around showing love through actions and acts of service. Actions like doing household chores, running errands, or performing thoughtful tasks for the other person are considered expressions of love for individuals with this love language.

3. **Receiving Gifts**: People with this love language feel most loved when they receive thoughtful gifts. It's not necessarily about the material value of the gift but rather the effort and thoughtfulness put into choosing it.

4. **Quality Time**: This love language involves spending quality time together and giving undivided attention. Engaging in meaningful conversations, shared activities, and simply being present and attentive are essential for individuals with this love language.

5. **Physical Touch**: This love language is all about expressing love through physical affection. Hugs, kisses, holding hands, and other forms of touch are

vital for people with this love language to feel loved and appreciated.

It's important to note that different people have different primary love languages and understanding and communicating in each other's love languages can lead to more fulfilling and satisfying relationships.

Understanding your love language will help you know how to position yourself for it.

Not everyone is meant to give you what you need; understand who is in your space to serve you.

And remember, if you don't get love, you can learn to give it, hence the need to always keep your love tank full.

- *Worth is not dependent on a change of circumstances or age. Example: You are worthy at every stage of life, regardless of your age.*

Never try to renew or refurbish your worth. You are not like a car that needs servicing after some time, neither does your worth go through the process of wear and tear. *Learn to adjust with the change of circumstances but keep yourself afloat from the reservoir of your self-worth.*

- *We set ourselves free when we recognize that worth is not measured by what we put into it. Worth is just IT. Worth is worth in and of itself.*

It's your worth so others have nothing to do with it. What you choose to do with it will determine how much you reap from it. Worth is not a feeling but a state of being that is derived from the source of your being who is your creator. Stop putting standards on your worth and begin to treasure it. When you do that, you acknowledge that nothing is missing.

- *Knowing you are enough is the first step to celebrating yourself.*

Learn to appreciate and be kind to yourself. If you become your number one fan, you will be surprised at how much others will begin to celebrate you.

1. **Be your number one fan:** Just as it is not fair to be the first critic to yourself, practice being the first one to give yourself an applause for the little steps you make. When others applause you it just adds to confirm what you already know.

2. **Internal gauge:** Ask yourself questions that lead you to reflect on your specific goals rather than focusing on what others have done. You are unique in how you deliver therefore even if you tried to copy and paste there will be a disconnect from the original. *'Be original yourself'*.

3. **Notice what excites you:** What things do you do that put a smile on your face? What activities do you do that bring you joy and fulfilment intrinsically? What places do you go that make you feel refreshed?

4.   **Manage what takes your attention:** While social media is good, it can be a trigger of feeling inadequate. Manage the time you give to social media and balance it with what builds you. You can practice parenting yourself by making the right choices.

5.   **Read your book:** Everyone has a story to tell, and each story has chapters. Some chapters are full of victories and others have lessons. Learn to look at the victory pages more and celebrate the little or the many achievements so far.

Remember that building a strong sense of self-worth takes time and effort. Be patient with yourself as you work on reducing your dependence on external validation. There is room to still do better because there is always a tomorrow and God is in it waiting to usher you in.

For I know the plans I have for you," declares the LORD, "plans to prosper you and not to harm you, plans to give you hope and a future (Jeremiah 29:11).

Time to Reflect:

Name some ways you will start honouring yourself by intentionally giving yourself love. Use the above keywords to support your self-love bank.

If you don't get love, you can learn to give it, hence the need to always keep your love tank full.

- Pastor Judy Babu

Chapter SEVEN:

Your Worth is Intact and Irreversible

What are the key identifiers of your true worth?

- **You cannot redefine your worth, you can only discover it. It is already within you.**

Quit trying to look at others to understand you, you are incomparable because the space you occupy on earth will never be occupied by another, you don't have a copyright. You were born with a clean self-esteem and the measure of value you place on yourself will help sustain what is already in existence.

What you tell yourself daily will form your lifelong narrative. A Narrative is what helps tell your story. Learn not to listen to your critical voice which tends to stir up some feelings like shame, inabilities, mistakes which can be a mental punishment. Learn to be grateful each day and notice the difference that makes in your feelings.

- **Purpose to rise above the demeaning voice and begin to use what you have to make a difference.**

Four ways on how you can do that effectively.

1. Discover your heart desire - what change do you Want to make in the world?
2. Discover what stops you from making those changes – what type of a stop sign is Infront of you – is it people, fear, or unbelief?

3. Think through how your life would be if your heart's desires were manifested?
4. How would it be if you never achieve these desires?

- *You cannot compare your worth to anything. You are just you. Life experiences don't decrease your worth in value.*

Always remember that life events are inevitable, and they bring changes in ourselves. However, how we feel because of what has happened is not who we are. The divorce or separation you went through or the job you lost are not evidence that you are a bad person. Never try to interpret how you feel as your true self because that can easily produce distorted and inaccurate ways of thinking that can further impact on your self-worth. Don't feel like you are a failure. See your worth by looking beyond your externals. People are short-lived; your worth will outlive them.

Paul saw his past as a testimony of the faithfulness of God and the evidence of His grace and so when he spoke to the church in Galatians, he was not shy to publicly say who he was then was not who he was now. His perception of his past did not deter him from stepping into his purpose. The detour in Paul's journey to fulfilling his life's destiny was an essential step in his learning and self-discovery process.

For you have heard of my previous way of life in Judaism, how intensely I persecuted the church of God and tried to destroy it. I was advancing in

Judaism beyond many of my own age among my people and was extremely zealous for the traditions of my fathers. But when God, who set me apart from my mother's womb and called me by his grace, was pleased to reveal his Son in me so that I might preach him among the Gentiles, my immediate response was not to consult any human being. (Galatians 1:13-16)

- **You are not a victim of your past but a student of the lessons you have learned through your mistakes.**

Rewrite your story using those lessons and let people learn from your mistakes and save them from making the same mistakes.

Paul says in 1 Corinthians 13:11, *When I was a child, I thought like a child, but when I became a man, I put away childish things.*

Good parenting is when you can learn to parent and nurture the newfound person in you to navigate life through the destined path paved for you. Life can be enriched with your personal lived experience. Therefore, when mentors fail you, gift yourself with your own experience.

You are not a victim of your past.
You are a *student* of the lessons you have learned through your mistakes.
♡
- Pastor Judy Babu

Time to Reflect:

How will you gift and empower yourself from what you have learned or experienced?

What will you turn into a blessing and energy or fuel to take you to your next level of breakthrough?

How will you grow your confidence through reframing words that disempowered you?

Write 5 things you will start reframing today. Speak to them daily to shift your atmosphere and grow your sense of self-worth.

Life enhancers

Destiny helpers are life enhancers who come in different forms for different periods. It is important to recognise the exit of one destiny helper is not the end of your worth, is not tied to your worth or self-perception of your worth.

Everyone is on an assignment and the fact that you are not the only one on earth, those that come as destiny helpers may not hang around for long because they must do the same for others. Understanding that you are also on assignment and the quicker you discover the better because there is someone waiting for you to help them realise their own assignment. Remember your worth is what enhances what you do in your assignment. when you learn to value yourself, you begin to tap into your strengths and abilities, talents and gifts which help you excel in what you do as well as endure when tough times come.

Your self-worth is a tool to reboot yourself and connect with who you really are.

Our gifts are not for ourselves.
They are for everyone who touches
base with us and taps into the grace
upon our lives.

- Dr Jackie Samuels

How to remain steadfast in your worth even when circumstances change

Your resilience and tenacity can help you bounce back even when stretched beyond measure.

1. **Internal resource:** Your worth does not stretch rather it remains static and can help you regulate back. Practice recoiling back to the inner strength where God is the Source of everything that is. In formlessness He creates something out of nothing (Genesis 1:1-2-3) therefore external circumstances such as job status, financial success, or relationship status should not make you feel unworthy. Your intrinsic value goes beyond these external factors.

2. **Learn your language:** Everyone has a language they use to speak to themselves, either critical or nurturing. The sooner you know your language the quicker you master the temperatures inside. Keep looking at your personal scripts that remind you who you are such as "*I don't have to be perfect,*" or "*I am good enough.*" And change the narrative for your sake.

3. **Have CPD:** Do not settle on what you already know. Have a growth mindset through *Continuous*

Personal Development which is the belief that your abilities can expand to serve you and others better. See challenges as opportunities for learning and improvement, rather than as reflections of your worth.

4. **Be real:** You can only do so much at any given time. Use the ladder approach and know that you can't reach the top staircase without stepping on each level upwards. Appreciate every step in your journey of progress and learn to keep your own records of success.

5. **Purpose to be distinct:** It is in our difference that we make a difference. It's okay to be different. Sameness takes away diversity and colour which helps us celebrate God's creation. *God saw everything that He made, and behold it was very good and He validated it completely* (Genesis 1:31).

6. **Choose a mentor/coach/Pastor:** Learning to walk alongside someone who has the best interest and wants to see the best in you is helpful. Sometimes there are things you can't see but others can help you see. There are some things you know that others don't know; you just need someone to listen when talking about them.

Remain steadfast and remember that circumstances are ever-changing, but your self-worth is constant. By implementing these strategies, you can cultivate a resilient and positive outlook on yourself and your life.

When I work with my clients the one thing they say is '*I wish I had known this before, that circumstances are not the definers of life but opportunities to draw life.*'

Read Lisa's testimony and breakthroughs from our work together below.

Lisa's testimony

As a young adult having Pastor Judy as a mentor has really helped me grow a lot over the years. I have become more aware of myself in a world so diverse where anyone can become an influence. Having regular sessions has helped me understand myself and accept who I am while understanding my self-worth.

My friends and family have also noticed a positive change in my character which is a testimony of Pastor Judy's unique guidance and coaching in my life. I aim to continue to grow through life spiritually and mentally by implementing the lessons I continue to learn through my mentorship sessions.

One change I have experienced because of the sessions is realizing my calm nature and being comfortable knowing my presence is enough. In conversation, I now aim to listen when people speak without panicking about what to say next. This has changed the way I interact with strangers.

My biggest breakthrough is the freedom I feel when taking time to nurture myself and rest. I no longer feel guilty about taking time to rest. This has been a big issue for me in the past where I always felt the need to be active and work.

My confidence has grown in the sense that I am more aware of myself, and my abilities and I speak with more certainty.

I can now make conversation with strangers without overthinking and paying attention to what the person I'm conversing with has to say. This has made interacting with people more enjoyable. Therefore, I do not overanalyze what I'm going to say before and during interactions.

I would advise someone in my position that it is very important to be aware of your weaknesses or setbacks and address them. Try to practice self-improvement in the areas of concern. Find someone who is trustworthy to help guide you through your personal growth.

I am most grateful for the time taken to help me grow through our regular sessions. I have learned a lot about myself that I did not know prior to working with Pastor Judy. I am very grateful for the person I am becoming.

Lisa G

Chapter EIGHT:

Worth is to be Celebrated

Celebrating your progress is essential to growing your self-worth.

- **Celebrate every small step as you grow in your worth.**

Growing in your worth means becoming more aware of your own value. Nobody can tell you how much you value because nobody knows everything about you. God is the only all-wise God and through Him you can understand your value, hence becoming His treasured possession which then helps you see yourself as a treasure.

You shall also be a crown of glory in the hand of the Lord, and a royal diadem in the hand of your God. (Isaiah 62:3)

Celebrate every win. Empower your gratitude muscles intentionally.

Learning the act of gratitude helps promote and boost your self-esteem which in return affirms your worth. Always remember intentionality is purposing to see beyond the odds and identifying the good. Refuse to be stuck at mistakes and know you have a right to make mistakes. Focus on those things that are of good report, true, faithful, lovely, and pure; if there is anything praiseworthy, meditate upon those things.

Judgment is the greatest hindrance to self-worth.

- ***Reward yourself by lifting self-judgment and begin to accept you are enough.***

If God showed love to us while we were yet sinners, why should you be the first one to condemn yourself? Since you cannot change the past allow the present to prepare a better future and take the lessons of the past as reference points to do things differently. God's grace is available to reinstate you again and you need not buy it but receive it.

- ***Worth is not given by men, but it is to be celebrated by men.***

When you learn to celebrate your worth, it becomes attractive to those looking at you. Make your worth attractive by showing others how to treat you as you learn to celebrate yourself.

People should not try to make you worthy; they should discover who you are and begin to celebrate you.

God is within her; she will not fall; God will help her at break of day. (Psalm 46:5, NIV)

The Lord your God in your midst, the Mighty One, will save; He will rejoice over you with gladness, He will quiet you with His love, He will rejoice over you with singing. (Zephaniah 3:17, NKJV)

How to celebrate yourself.

Serving others with your gifts and strengths is a wonderful way to make a positive impact on the world and contribute to your wellbeing as well as others. Here are some tips to follow.

1.   **Know what your niche is**: Reflect on your distinct and unique talents, skills, and abilities. *Why are you cast down, O my soul? And why are you disquieted within me? Hope in God; for I shall yet praise Him, the help of my countenance and my God.* (Psalm 43:5). Consider what comes naturally for you and continue doing it. What would you say your passion is or what brings a smile on your face. What problem are you solving?

2.   **Find out what troubles you**: Are there times you pick on something that other people are not doing and you know what should be done? That could be your area of strength so step out, take the honours, and serve people. There is nothing as good as when you put your gift into action, you feel nourished.

3.   **Volunteer:** There is so much joy in giving back to the community you live, look for charities, non-profit organizations, or community initiatives that align with your interests and talents and abilities.

4.   **Make yourself know**: Look for places and settings that will help grow your gift. We all have

different gifts, according to the grace given to each of us. If your gift is prophesying, then prophecy in accordance with your faith, if it is serving do the same, it is teaching or encouraging, do likewise (Romans 12:6-8).

5.   **Giving**: Whatever you purpose in your heart to give will in return bring to you a sixty and a hundred-fold. Fill your basket by emptying through giving. Noone sows in vain, there is always a harvest attached to your seed. Consider making donations to causes that are important to you.

6.   **Understudy**: Become a mentor by choosing somebody you can share your knowledge and wisdom with. Help them to discover their own gifts and abilities. It is fulfilling to see others thriving in your care and mentorship. Also help them to identify where their strengths lie in a particular area.

7.   **Purpose to be original**: If no one is doing what you want done, quit asking who can do it and be the initiator. An idea is birthed by one person but can be made alive by many others. Celebrate your dream and let that dream set a pace for others to build on.

8.   **Family community**: You are where you are at such a time like this to make a difference. Understand your environment and connect with those in your community by purposing to serve and engage them.

9.   **Have lasting commitment**: Stay in touch with what brings fulfilment and refrain from disconnection to your assignment. let your acts of

giving be tied to a routine so that there is more and meaningful impact.

10. **Encourage people**: Be a motivator by setting an example to those around you to use their gifts and strengths for positive change as well. Encourage your friends, family, and colleagues to join you in giving back.

Remember, giving back doesn't have to be grandiose or high-profile. Small acts of kindness and thoughtful contributions can make a significant difference in the lives of others. Embrace the idea of using your gifts to create a better world, and you'll find fulfilment in your efforts to give back.

Give Back: Use your talents and resources to help others. Contributing to the wellbeing of others can also reinforce your sense of worth and purpose.

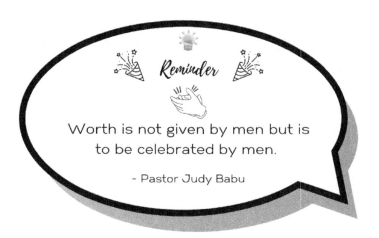

Reminder

Worth is not given by men but is to be celebrated by men.

- Pastor Judy Babu

Time to Reflect:

How does your '*authentic self*' manifest to others?

What do people like about you being in their space?

What have you identified that you can bring to the table of originality? Refer to your gifts, skills, affinities, and natural abilities that you will use to serve others and create deeper breakthroughs.

Giving back with your gifts and strengths is a wonderful way to make a positive impact on the world and contribute to the well-being of others.

- Pastor Judy Babu

Chapter NINE:

Worth is Not an Action

Consider this:

- It is not what we can or can't do that makes us worthy. Who we are is our worth.
- Don't look at your inability or limited ability as a yardstick as a definer of the level of your worth.
- We are not a product, we are human. You don't have to produce to feel worthy. Just BE.
- Worth is a state of your being. Being in the present moment is key to showcasing your worth. Hence your existence is valuable because no one else can occupy your space.
- Staying in the present moment enhances our worth.
- You can be present and not say much. Your presence will speak what words cannot say because presence comes with its own aura. That aura emanates from your internal point of reference where your goodness resides. Your goodness is wrapped up in your worth, creating a conducive environment that helps people acknowledge and appreciate their own worth.

Endeavor to remember and embrace the following elements as a bridge to maintaining your sense of being as the core foundation of your worth.

1. **Value**: Worth is a state of being that reflects the inherent significance or importance of an individual or object.

2. **Deserving**: Worth implies being deserving of attention, respect, or consideration because one's qualities, actions, or contributions.

3. **Merit**: Worth can be seen as the level of merit or worthiness someone possesses, based on their achievements, skills, or character.

4. **Self-esteem**: Worth is closely related to a person's self-esteem and self-perception, influencing how they view themselves and their capabilities.

5. **Dignity**: Worth can be equated with dignity, indicating that every individual possesses an intrinsic value regardless of external factors.

6. **Significance**: Worth signifies the extent to which someone or something is important or meaningful in each context.

7. **Pricelessness**: Worth can be described as priceless, representing something that cannot be adequately measured in monetary terms.

8. **Empowerment**: Recognizing one's worth can lead to a sense of empowerment and confidence in navigating life's challenges.

9. **Uniqueness**: Worth acknowledges the individuality and uniqueness of each person, highlighting their special qualities and contributions.

10. **Personal growth**: Understanding and embracing one's worth can foster personal growth and a sense of purpose in life.

Apply these ten tips and remember how priceless and unique you truly are.

Time to Reflect:

Can you think of some ways you will apply these secrets going forward? Write them below.

_____

_____

_____

_____

_____

_____

_____

_____

_____

_____

_____

_____

_____

_____

_____

_____

_____

_____

_____

_____

_____

Sharon's testimony

One of the changes I experienced through working with Judy is addressing unhealed trauma from a place of cultural competence. It enabled me to be a better mother and professional in my work.

My biggest breakthrough was ending the cycle of existing in toxic relationships and starting to build healthy relationships. Now I am self-fulfilled with a better understanding of myself and how to co-exist with others. These breakthroughs have greatly improved my relationships and outcomes in career and business.

As my confidence has grown, I have also learned how to ground my internal emotions no matter what is happening externally. This has made me an effective leader and holistic mentor. Best of all, I now have a sense of internal peace through life's changing circumstances and seasons.

I can thrive and succeed in most areas of my life by having successful relationships at home, work, and business. Now I can try new experiences and find it easier to deal with crises and remain grounded because of my healing. Previously, I was very anxious before, emotional to a point of breakdown and would lash out if in crises. This made me a hard person to relate with.

My advice to persons struggling with self-worth issues is to choose Judy because she covers all holistic areas of life. I felt that she culturally understood me and helped me understand how to posture myself in a western society. I would therefore encourage women from all backgrounds to work with her if you want to live life and thrive holistically. In relationships, work, career, faith, culture, and money. She has taught me to love, live, and succeed exceedingly, thrive in relationships, and enjoy life unapologetically. I no longer survive but thrive in all I do.

Sharon Gitau

Chapter TEN:

Worth is Not Given in Droplets Waiting to be Filled in by Someone Else

You already have within you the river of worth. Open it, access it, embrace it, OWN IT, and then share it. You cannot share or give what you don't have. Nobody else has it because your uniqueness is what should serve others. Your service should not stop at yourself otherwise ego kicks in; serve through the content you are sharing. You cannot embrace what you do not acknowledge or appreciate.

I want to reference a story in the Bible of two ladies who waited for one another to fill in so they would feel enough.

> *Leah became pregnant and gave birth to a son. She named him Reuben, for she said, "It is because the LORD has seen my misery. Surely my husband will love me now." She conceived again, and when she gave birth to a son she said, "Because the LORD heard that I am not loved, he gave me this one too." So she named him Simeon. Again she conceived, and when she gave birth to a son she said, "Now at last my husband will become attached to me, because I have borne him three sons." So he was named Levi. She conceived again, and when she gave birth to a son she said, "This time I will praise the LORD." So, she named him Judah. Then she*

stopped having children. (Genesis 29:32-35, NIV)

Leah was desperate about her empty love tank, and she longed for her husband to fill in some drops of love. Not that love from a husband is bad; don't get me wrong, every married person deserves it. But what Leah was implying here was that she needed to do something for her husband to love her. She felt there was a missing link and the sooner that gap was sealed the quicker she could get her husband back. Leah's okay-ness was in childbearing. You notice that she used her children as bait for attachment, rather than counting them as blessings in her own life. I wonder if she got to enjoy the firstborn because each child served a specific purpose.

- Don't use your deserving blessing to be bait for winning love. Let love find you as you are.
- *If you were a guru and you were advising Leah what not to do, what would you say to her?*

- *As a mother, if Leah was your daughter, what nugget would you share with her about womanhood?*

- *As a dad, if Leah was your daughter, what secret would you share with her about manhood?*

- *If you found yourself in this position, how would you regulate or ground yourself?*

When Rachel saw that she was not bearing Jacob any children, she became jealous of her sister. So she said to Jacob, "Give me children, or I'll die!" Jacob became angry with her and said, "Am I in the place of God, who has kept you from having children?" Then she said, "Here is Bilhah, my servant. Sleep with her so that she can bear children for me and I too can build a family through her."

So she gave him her servant Bilhah as a wife. Jacob slept with her, and she became pregnant and bore him a son. Then Rachel said, "God has vindicated me; he has listened to my plea and given me a son." Because of this she named him Dan. Rachel's servant Bilhah conceived again and bore Jacob a second son. Then Rachel said, "I have had a great struggle with my sister, and I have won." So she named him Naphtali. (Genesis 30:1-8)

Remember we said that nobody makes you feel because your feelings are your own. ***Rachel's jealousy came because of her internal frame of reference***. Although she was beautiful and loved by her husband, she had serious insecurity issues because of Leah. She wanted Leah to remain in her status quo as from the beginning because that gave her confidence that she was going to remain the favourite.

I presume when Rachel saw the love given to Leah, she got worried of losing the droplets of love from her husband that kept her afloat. So over and above what she had earned she found herself in the trap of comparison and decided to use the same bait (her own blessed children) to win love back to herself.

The two sisters did not understand each other's internal conflicts surrounding their marriage to the same man. By comparing each other's seeming 'blessing', each negated their own unique gift which in turn led them to devalue their own sense of self-worth.

At this point I want to pause and ask you:

Do you sometimes find yourself using something to win love? If so, what is your bait? And has it worked so far or do you feel like you need to keep doing it?

Rachel's worldview was that life without the droplets of love was not worth living.

She linked her life's worth to having children otherwise she was not worth living.

Have you ever felt like you have been dragged into affairs that help to win battles of worthlessness?

Bilhah found herself in this drama where Rachel's need of love preceded her worth.

Time to Reflect:

- I ask again: If you had a chance to have a one to one with Rachel, what would you say to her?

- If you were the man in this drama, how would you help these two girls?

- What do you think the husband in this drama was gaining from these two girls that prevented him from addressing and resolving the conflict?

Embracing Individuality: Your lived experience contributes to your unique skills and perspectives that no one else possesses. Embrace your individuality and celebrate the things that make you different from others. Understanding that you have a distinct contribution to offer to the world reinforces your sense of worth.8. Identify and master the symptoms that make you dependent on people for worth.

Insecurity: Feeling insecure compromises your worth. When you lack proper attachment from people you latch onto often leads to insecurity and chasing after love. You can give yourself what others have refused to give you. You can be your own guardian, learning to parent the part of you that is still feeling neglected and lonely. Acknowledge the void and remember that what happened in the past has no power to your future because you have today and that can be the beginning of discovering what is available and accessible to fill that void.

Reframe: You are a full measure of your total worth. You are not waiting to be good; you are already good. Stop being unkind to yourself and start being compassionate. Practice Saying positive things about yourself and do the things that you enjoy.

Avoid the tendency to compare yourself with others. If you can avoid spending a lot of time on social media and use the time to invest in yourself, you might surprise yourself with how much can come from you. Remember what people display about their status in life is not always the full picture.

Enjoy discovering yourself and taking the journey of self-awareness to help you create the right portrait of yourself. People liking you should be a bonus. Their liking should be confirmation of what you already know. Quit proving your self-worth. *You are IT*.

People-pleasing syndrome is an enemy of our worth. People-pleasing keeps one in a dangerous cycle of living people's lives at the expense of your own authenticity.

- Start focusing on your achievements and begin the habit of praising yourself.
- Celebrating your successes shifts your mind from focusing on others.
- Accept every compliment that comes your way, especially from people you think have the best interest at heart and use that to boost your morale.
- Become conscious of the impact you make in people's lives because nobody else can do what you do.
- Your journal should have a page with things you like about yourself.

Co-dependence drags one into vulnerability leading to becoming a doormat. Be yourself. Know that you are enough. Find your safe place in God and remember your dependence on God is what should serve you because God has the template of your life and He desires that you thrive Release the need to always get the approval of others before making a final decision that affects your wellbeing, growth, empowerment…

Listening to what others say about certain areas for self-growth can help you release self-condemnation. Then you will access your true worth with ease and grace.

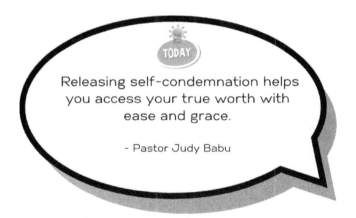

TODAY

Releasing self-condemnation helps you access your true worth with ease and grace.

- Pastor Judy Babu

Chapter ELEVEN:

The Root of Worthlessness

The *deception of the missing link* is the hook to worthlessness. Genesis 1 – The serpent came to Eve and deceived her. He used a *lie hook* to win her into the lie that she was not good enough until she got something else. She started doubting her *'enough-Ness'* and began searching for what was lacking. Self-doubt creates a conducive ground to feel worthless. **The remedy for self-doubt** is self-affirmations, meditation on God's Word and speaking the Word to yourself intentionally. Realize that what we focus on expands, therefore focus on your strengths and what you are good at and excel in it.

Significant others also affect how we feel about ourselves because growing up we depended on them (parents, siblings, teachers, bosses, spouses, friends). Sometimes the replayed tracks from people close to us create discord that disempowers our self-worth and stifles our growth. They should not hold us hostage to our worth **because we now know better.**

Unbelief. Lack of self-belief becomes the engine that drives our thoughts and actions, leading to living inauthentically (example: keeping up with the Joneses). Your *'good enough'* vibe should come from understanding your existence and that no one else can occupy the space you occupy now or in the future.

Nobody will ever be you.

Be gentle and don't add what you were not meant to have in the first place. This might give you extra work to maintain it. Be content and comfortable with what you found when you arrived on earth.

Overcoming feelings of worthlessness is a common struggle for many people. Thankfully, the Bible offers valuable guidance and encouragement to address these emotions. Let us now examine nine biblical principles to help conquer the deception of worthlessness.

1. **Your true identity:** Understand that as a believer, your worth is not based on your achievements or failures but on being a child of God. Embrace passages like Ephesians 2:10 that remind you that you are God's workmanship, created for good works.

2. **Renew your mind:** Regularly meditate on Scripture to combat negative thoughts. Romans 12:2 encourages us to be transformed by the renewing of our minds, which can help replace feelings of worthlessness with God's Truth.

3. **Spiritual discipline:** Take your feelings of worthlessness to God in prayer. Philippians 4:6-7 reminds us to *present* our *requests to God with thanksgiving, and His peace will guard* our *hearts and minds.*

4. **Connect to the Rock:** Recognize that you can do all things through Christ who strengthens you (Philippians 4:13). Trust in God's power rather than relying solely on your abilities.

5. **Take charge of your space:** Seek out a supportive community of believers who can encourage you and hold you accountable. Proverbs 27:17 teaches that *iron sharpens iron.*

6. **Serve:** Engaging in acts of service can help shift the focus from your worthlessness to meeting the needs of others. Jesus taught us that serving others is a key aspect of following Him. *...just as the Son of Man did not come to be served, but to serve, and to give His life a ransom for many."* (Matthew 20:28). Also, in 1 Peter 4:10 (NIV), *Each of you should use whatever gift you have received to serve others, as faithful stewards of God's grace in its various forms.*

7. **True Love:** Meditate on the depth of God's Love for you. Romans 5:8 reminds us that *while we were still sinners, Christ died for us,* demonstrating His unconditional love. Additionally, Ephesians 3:17-19 exhorts us, *that Christ may dwell in your hearts through faith; that you, being rooted and grounded in love, may be able to comprehend with all the saints what is the width and length and depth and height—to know the love of Christ which passes knowledge; that you may be filled with all the fullness of God.*

8. **Let go:** Holding onto guilt and unforgiveness can contribute to feelings of worthlessness. Embrace the forgiveness offered through Christ and extend it to others. Ephesians 4:32 states, *And be kind to one another, tenderhearted, forgiving one another, even as God in Christ forgave you.*

9. **Manage expectations:** Acknowledge that you are not perfect and that it's okay to make mistakes. Embrace grace and remember that God's strength is made perfect in our weaknesses. *And He said to me, "My grace is sufficient for you, for My strength is made perfect in weakness." Therefore most gladly I will rather boast in my infirmities, that the power of Christ may rest upon me* (2 Corinthians 12:9).

Remember that overcoming feelings of worthlessness is a journey that may take time and effort. Be patient with yourself and trust in God's transformative power to change your perspective.

Free It. Unlock Your Self-worth.

Chapter TWELVE:

The Journey to Recovery

Realigning with who you are and owning your worth takes time, determination, and consistency. Embrace these five steps to recovery and growth.

- **Self-acceptance** awards you with the propelling energy to soar to great heights like an eagle. Nothing brings the eagle down except by its will. Be Unstoppable. The choice you make gives power to your feelings which then depend on your thoughts for instruction so they can act. Examine your strengths. The eagle is identified by its ability to maximize its flight. *But those who wait on the Lord shall renew their strength; they shall mount up with wings like eagles, they shall run and not be weary, they shall walk and not faint* (Isaiah 40:31). You must be honest with yourself and acknowledge what you cannot do and be okay with it. Remember you cannot do everything.

- **Self-forgiveness** is the healing gift that no one can give you. It is within your reach to obtain it when you become aware of the stains it leaves in your inner self. Accept your mistakes and learn from them; serve others by teaching them through your mistakes and let what you see as bad become your testimony of your transformation. Learn to be compassionate to yourself and always find ways of self-soothing. Remember if someone else was asking for your forgiveness you would graciously forgive them. If you were the one asking for forgiveness, would you rather drown yourself in condemnation or receive the gift?

- **Self-love:** Refuels itself from the Source of all things – God. It serves you in the presence of rejection, hatred, hostility, dismissal, where you are uncelebrated. Self-love should come from the understanding that God has no rejects and if you are part of creation then in God's eyes you are good for everything, He created was good. Practice silences the critical voice by lifting the condition for your deserving love.

- **Empathy**. Self-empathy invites you to listen to your nurturing voice that affirms who you really are. If no one can understand you, God can and He has this to say, *"Come now, and let us reason together,"* *Says the Lord, "Though your sins are like scarlet,* *they shall be as white as snow; though they are red* *like crimson, they shall be as wool.* (Isaiah 1:18). Sometimes people fail to understand because their capacity to listen is blurred by their own issues. Be the first to understand yourself, lower your expectation and standard. Empathy is a sign that you believe what you are trying to say is true. It's okay not to be okay. Acknowledge you are on a journey, and you need to intentionally support yourself in the self-worth process. **Be your #1 fan**. Be mindful: when people are criticizing you, refuse to be the second person criticizing yourself.

- **Genuineness:** Be honest with yourself. Accept what you are not able to do and be content. Know that what you can already do is great. You are a work in progress just like the next person. Remember what you cannot do somebody else will do. There is a divine synergy in operation, and this can only be effective and impactful if you allow yourself to remain in your lane and only do you. We are all created with freedom to be real and authentic and until we acknowledge it, access it and enjoy it we will always think somebody else should free us.

XO's testimony

When I first contacted Pastor Judy in 2018 I was overwhelmed with guilt, shame, and the consequences of sin over choices made as a young adult.

Although I had studied Scripture and listened to my parents obediently for many years, I made some regrettable mistakes that created a feeling of unworthiness. With no one to turn to, I spiralled into despair from deep shame, fear, anxiety, and uncertainty. For the first time in my life, I could not feel God's presence in my life.

A desperate broken vessel, I turned to Pastor Judy for help. She understood and lovingly helped me to seek God's forgiveness. She guided me to understand confession and repentance, and above all reminded me of God's loving and faithful nature. Step by step, I started learning about our loving Father; through Pastor Judy's counselling and prayers, I returned to Church.

Before long, an unexpected storm reared its ugly head. My husband of 6 years at the time confessed that he had been unfaithful to me multiple times during our marriage. My world shattered again at this confession as the disempowering wounds and feelings resurfaced. Thankfully, God led me back to Pastor Judy and we started working together again. At the time, I struggled to believe I would ever find healing, peace, forgiveness, and joy. Pastor Judy's wise counsel helped me overcome my darkest despair. She introduced me to the meaning of self-love and lovingly encouraged me to find my footing as the girl God created for His purposes.

DX's transformational journey...

I thank God for healing my brokenness and for reminding me that if I was the lost sheep, He would leave the 99 to find me. He healed my past, forgave my wrong choices, and washed my sins with the blood of Jesus. Now I am a new creation. As I started accepting God's truth about me as His beloved daughter, I forgave my husband and let go of all the negative thoughts that had been crowding my mind in pain and despair. I had my miracle of forgiveness which removed the darkness that had overshadowed my world.

My dad lovingly doted on me and built my confidence. When my confidence and self-esteem were shattered, Pastor Judy's counselling helped me regain my self-confidence. As a result, I would have shied away from many things I'm now able to confront head-on. I'm now able to be assertive over things that concern me and others.

I'm forever grateful for all the love and guidance Pastor Judy has tirelessly provided for me. She reminded me of Christ's love for me, His unwavering presence in my life and above all, there is no hole deep enough that I can ever hide from Him. She taught me about self-love which I had never heard of before her lessons. Understanding that I am a work in progress and God's grace is sufficient for all my needs keeps me well grounded.

Word of encouragement...

Understanding God's love for you and His unwavering faithfulness should remind you that He is for you. He sees your tears, He knows your deepest pain and through it all, He's got you. Believe it, hold onto it because it is true.

DX

Six remedies to rediscover your worth

Rediscovering your worth is an important journey of self-discovery and self-acceptance. Here are six remedies to help you along the way:

Look after yourself: Be kind and compassionate to yourself, especially during difficult times. Acknowledge your imperfections and treat yourself with the same understanding and care you would offer a friend.

Let your passion evolve: Make a list of your skills, talents, and achievements. Focus on the positive aspects of yourself and recognize the unique qualities that make you special.

Create your growth ladder: Break down larger aspirations into smaller, achievable steps. Celebrate each accomplishment, no matter how minor, as they all contribute to your sense of worth.

Erase self-comparisons: Avoid comparing yourself to others, as this can lead to feelings of inadequacy. Instead, focus on your personal growth and progress. You will discover the richness within you that can be emulated. Paul said in 1 Corinthians 11:1, *Follow my example, as I follow the example of Christ.* Emulate the richness within you which is Christ Himself.

Define your relationships: Spend time with people who celebrate you and can smell the roses in your presence. People who support and uplift you desire the best for you. Therefore, avoid toxic relationships that undermine your self-esteem.

Pursue enjoyable interests: Engage in activities you love to boost your self-esteem. Hobbies that bring you joy and a sense of fulfilment lead to your purpose-driven life in the spirit of excellence.

God works with what we already have, not what we don't have or don't love. He empowers our gifts in so many ways.

Self-reflection questions:

Can you think of 5 things you do effortlessly that make you smile?

My personal examples: I love listening to people express their emotions and thoughts. My passion is to see people thrive and attain the freedom within to do what they have always wanted to do.

- What do you already do to help others for free that you can be paid for?

Everyone has been entrusted with diverse gifts and talents. Your gift is what makes room for you and ushers you into your destiny.

- What are your gifts/talents/skills/abilities?

Identify your gifts:

#1. Where you are.

- Your roots (e.g. public speaking, teaching, nursing, preaching, mentoring…)

- Who are you called to? (e.g. small groups, ladies cooking/sewing club, men's youth programs, other…)

- How are you empowering your gifts? (e.g. Writing a book, podcasting, YouTubing, blogging, social presence, online/offline mentorship)

#2. Your destination.

- What are your strengths? (Your God-given assignment, purpose, niche).

Evidence that you are arriving at your destination:

Embrace fulfilment: This manifests when you are aligned with God's will and purpose for your life.

Our dreams and visions are valid and never in vain. They are given to us to bring out God's flavour and fruitfulness in others and ourselves. As God's habitation, let us walk in obedience to His Will, Purpose, and Timing.

Understanding our dreams would deeply enrich others. However, sometimes we limit others by not living our dreams and assignments. Apply these four secrets to deepen your breakthroughs by owning your dreams and visions.

Be daily grateful: Take note of things that have enlightened your day. Journalling can keep you on track of intentional moments of gratitude which you can later reflect on and give thanks for manifested breakthroughs. Doing this can help shift your focus from perceived shortcomings to the positive aspects of your life.

What is your favourite gratitude journal type? Some people favor bullet journals (bujo) and use them to record grateful moments in bullet format.

Questioning negative thoughts: When negative thoughts arise, question their validity. Replace them with positive affirmations and remind yourself of your strengths. It often helps to record your reframing truths in your journal because thoughts are seeds which grow.

Therefore, releasing negative thoughts creates space for positive realities to manifest easily.

Access professional help when necessary: Start by discovering the source of your need. You know you have arrived at your destination when you are able to articulate your needs and access the right resources. If you're struggling with deep-seated issues, consider speaking with a therapist or counsellor who can provide guidance and support.

Give yourself first place: You empower your self-growth when you identify the recipe for your soul's wellbeing. Nurture your physical, emotional, and mental well-being. Love yourself as you love others (Matthew 22:39; Mark 12:31). Make rest a priority without apology and take yourself to a retreat. Eat nutritious food, exercise regularly, and engage in mindfulness practices to cultivate a sense of inner peace and worth.

Remember, *rediscovering your worth is a process that takes time and effort. Be patient with yourself and trust that you are worthy of love, respect, and happiness, just as you are*.

PART TWO:

Remedies To Empower Your Self-Worth

Let us now uncover ten remedies that will help you grow your self-worth as you align with your God-given role and purpose on earth. You are called to shine in your identity as a uniquely created child of God.

Chapter THIRTEEN:

Ten Ingredients For Building Self-Worth And Walking In Divine Purpose

Your God given task matches who you are. Stepping into your assignment and purpose is the only thing that can bring fulfilment in your life. God is your Masterpiece and the intrinsic you is a representation of God on earth. If you can allow yourself to serve others, you will be letting God enrich mankind with His giftedness.

OBEDIENCE: To believe what you really are and own it. Do you sometimes struggle with obeying a directive when someone in authority asks you to do something that goes against your natural inclination?

FREEDOM: Without freedom you cannot be your true self. Freedom makes you human. It helps you to make your own choices. Freedom helps you to choose your personal path which then calls favour and responsibility to follow the path. *Have you been happy with the way your life is*?

My personal motto is '***FREE IT***'. I believe there is something we wish to disconnect from so we can live. Name your 'IT'.

WE ARE ALL CREATED WITH FREEDOM.

However, when we don't acknowledge it, we limit what we can achieve with the gifts God has deposited in us. Placing limitations on ourselves often happens because of doubt, fear, and not feeling good enough.

KINDNESS: Kindness invites you to share something good you like about another. Complimenting one another brightens their day. *When was the last time you made someone feel like they matter*?

GENTLENESS: embracing the gentle side of ourselves helps to acknowledge our strong and weak parts. There is power in being gentle to yourself. The gentle side can easily be mistaken as the shadow side, which can hinder our progress. *How often do you listen to the inner tune*? That's where personal power emanates from.

COMPASSION: Give yourself a break. Compassion is like a muscle that is strengthened when you engage in daily exercise. Choose compassion over judgment. Treat yourself with compassion and help yourself to arrive at better self-appraisal.

JOYFULNESS: *Can happiness lead to confidence?* Yes, confidence is when one belief in oneself and happiness has to do with the whole life reaching a sense of becoming. Happiness is empowered when one is satisfied with their life. *When was the last time you enjoyed contentment?*

GRATEFULNESS: If you want to change your perception and world view, begin to be grateful each day. There must be something you liked today. Fight envy and regret by being grateful. *Do you keep a journal and what is in it?*

GENEROSITY: This is a natural repellent of self-hate. When we learn to gift ourselves with good things, we confirm that we are valuable. *When was the last time you treated yourself out?*

PATIENCE: Be patient with yourself and promote self-growth and self-worth. Bear with your past mistakes and learn to be resilient. How often do you say to yourself*: 'A little longer will always pay off'*? Imagine being stuck in traffic and the person behind you keeps honking. Of course, this will stir up anger and frustration and will end up serving you negatively. Say, 'Good things come to those who wait'. *How long can you wait?*

HONOUR: *How will you honour yourself? Is dignity a priority for you?* Live your life in authenticity and ***enjoy you*** as you walk through life. ***Are you your number one fan?***

Self-reflection Exercise:

The following reflection teaser questions will help you become more aware of some blockages that sometimes keep you stuck when you are trying to achieve the above breakthroughs.

Where do the above corresponding keywords fit in the questions below?

- How do you know you are obedient to shouts of your true self?

- When was the last time you cared less what everyone thinks about you?

- Do you sometimes wish you could blow your own trumpet without feeling guilty that you appear arrogant or prideful?

- How do you soothe the part of you that can't do much, or when was the last time you had a conversation with your weaker part of self?

- What do you do when you are happy? How does that manifest outwardly?

- When was the last time you rewarded yourself for doing good? What was the reward?

- What kind of environment do you create for the value in you to thrive?

- How do you regulate the expectations you have on yourself? Does the statement '*I am a work in progress*' ever surface?

It is time to embrace your self-worth. ***Free it. Access it. Enjoy It.***

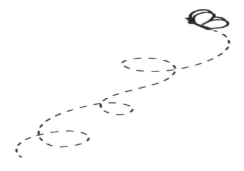

Final Thoughts

In conclusion…

I have fought the good fight and ran the race. Now awaits the crown of righteousness… There are many more who will receive the crown as they walk in freedom in Christ, having understood their self-worth.

Our gifts are not for ourselves. They are for everyone who touches base with us and taps into the grace upon our lives. - Dr Jacqueline Samuels

When you discover what and who you are and tap into your gifts, you begin to serve others. That's when you live a life of *purpose* which is all about serving others, not yourself.

Every good gift and every perfect gift is from above, and comes down from the Father of lights, with whom there is no variation or shadow of turning. Of His own will He brought us forth by the word of truth, that we might be a kind of firstfruits of His creatures. (James 1:17-18)

Therefore the Lord will wait, that He may be gracious to you; and therefore, He will be exalted, that He may have mercy on you. For the Lord is a God of justice; blessed are all those who wait for Him. (Isaiah 30:18)

Serena's testimony

Pastor Judy has been a great support in my life, especially in discovering my self-worth. I say this because of the amazing growth I have experienced in the many areas I previously struggled in.

One major change over the years has centred around thoughts about me. During my late teens, I noticed my thoughts were primarily negative. I felt different as though no one understood me. I felt alone which filled me with trepidation. A negative cycle of self-criticism, low self-esteem, self-hate, and more followed, all while trying to pinpoint what exactly was wrong with me. I was desperate to try and make sense of what I was going through and overcome this great fear.

It was during this very dark time when I reached out to Pastor Judy. During our sessions together she helped me understand more about what I was experiencing. The long-anticipated desire to understand myself was finally uncovered; this breath of fresh air felt like my life had just begun.

The turning point that led to my breakthrough came when I discovered the erroneous belief core belief within myself that 'something was wrong with me'. There was never anything wrong with me. However, allowing inferior thoughts to take over caused me to believe that having negative past life experiences meant that something was wrong with me and that everyone else was living a happy, fulfilled life full of high self-esteem, purpose, and positivity.

Thoughts of trying to unveil why I was never happy but always anxious, fearful, and timid were finally put to rest. I realized that I had been trying to erase my past rather than coming to terms with what made me who I am today. I would overthink things and do everything in my power to question why I was like that and attempt to suppress everything I didn't like. Little did I know that was the wrong approach which had caused my low self-esteem to spiral.

Serena's Transformations

By working with Pastor Judy, I learned how to accept and embrace everything about myself. She guided me on how to turn negative thoughts into positive ones, taught me how to unlearn unhealthy patterns, and a lot more. I had never felt so empowered and in charge of my own life before. My self-confidence grew and I began to be unapologetically me. I finally understood the meaning of self-worth which slowly started to erase the deep-rooted feelings of fear. Standing on my own beliefs that I am imperfectly perfect and enough, I overcame the need to fit in and be accepted to feel 'normal. The moment I no longer felt the need to seek validation was when I knew something within me had changed for the better, something I probably would not have been able to achieve without the sessions.

I have now been able to accept who I am, instead of internalizing the bad and pretending to be okay. Whenever I backslide and slip into the old negative patterns, I overcome them by applying the tips Pastor Judy taught me. For example, I have the confidence to now catch a negative thought in the process and identify why it is there rather than avoiding it.

Before I would allow a negative thought to lead me to self-criticism or try to protect myself from the 'worst case scenario'. She also taught me that everyone experiences negative thoughts at some point in life, and we can either choose to water the negative thoughts when they come or challenge them with the truth by affirming ourselves.

Although I am still a work in progress, I am very grateful to Pastor Judy for walking with me through a difficult time and for the great work she is doing to help me. I have never felt judged or misunderstood in her presence. I am also grateful to myself for taking that leap of faith to seek help. And above all, I am most grateful to God for opening a door to turn my life around and discover my self-worth.

If I could advise anyone in my position, it would be that vulnerability is your greatest strength. If you are in a place of hopelessness, remember that there is nothing else to lose, therefore the best starting point is to be open, honest, and vulnerable. Do not let thoughts of feeling judged or looking 'weak' overcome the possibility of discovering your self-worth. You are more than capable of winning the battle in your mind.

Serena G

Conclusion: Prospects

I am excited about the trajectory this book has taken because I see it serving people who consciously wish to *get InTouch with self*. Every one of us has at one point in life been caught up in a rut wondering or questioning who we are. To some, finding self has resulted in reframing or rewriting their stories.

To others, it has meant accepting the status quo and settling for convenience's sake. Either way the greatest miracle is trusting that nothing is outside of us. If we are ready to get in touch with ourselves and help others do the same, *share this book's ISBN:* **9798860172418.** Help your contacts to get their copy of this guide and reconnect with the concealed self. This manual is also a perfect reference guide for whenever the dark clouds hover.

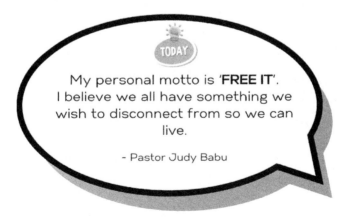

TODAY

My personal motto is '**FREE IT**'. I believe we all have something we wish to disconnect from so we can live.

- Pastor Judy Babu

About the Author

Judy Babu holds a Bachelor of Arts degree in Theology and a level 6 in Counselling and Psychotherapy. She is a member of the British Association of Counsellors and Psychotherapists (BACP). The author serves as a psychotherapeutic practitioner and is a Community Coach and Trainer for Community ambassadors.

Judy Babu resides in Swindon UK and currently serves as an associate Pastor at Bible Life Fellowship alongside her husband Pastor Timothy Babu. The author is mother to Kevin & Lynette and grandma to Ezrah.

Let's connect:

Website: **www.freeit.org.uk**

Email: **judyfreeit@gmail.com**

Gratefully,

Pastor Judy

Printed in Great Britain
by Amazon

36752238R00069